THE COMING TRIAL

YOU CANNOT ESCAPE IT

A.A.O. OLATUNDE

The coming trial: you cannot escape it

ISBN: 978-0-9560398-6-6

Published by A.A.O. Olatunde
www.thechristianfoundationbooks.com

CONTENTS

Chapter 1

THE DEFENDANT

At the end of this age, every person that has ever lived will face a trial. It is a very important trial in the programme of God: "And as it is appointed unto men once to die, but after this the judgment..." (Hebrews 9:27).

There will be a great resurrection:

"And many of them that sleep in the dust of the earth shall awake, some to everlasting life, and some to shame *and* everlasting contempt." Daniel 12:2

After the great resurrection, the coming trial will commence. The outcomes of the trial will determine the endless end of every person: good (I Corinthians 3:13-14) or bad, comfortable or painful, delightful or disastrous.

Even during earthly lifetime, before everybody's big day, Satan and his company keep accusing people on account of their sins and wrong doings, so as to cause the withdrawal of God's blessings, and to allow his cruelty.

John said, "And I heard a loud voice saying in heaven, Now is come salvation, and strength, and the kingdom of our God, and the power of his Christ: for the accuser of our brethren is cast down, which accused them before our God day and night" (Revelation 12:10). The accuser of the brethren is Satan and his company.

Satan and his company have already been judged for their rebellion against God. God has already given them His sentence. They are not waiting for a trial. They are waiting for their sentence to be carried out. This is their endless end: "And the devil that deceived them was cast into the lake of fire" (Revelation 20:10).

Because their end has already been determined, they want to do damage, as soon as possible, as much as possible, as terrible as possible. They seek legal grounds to work through the use of temptations and deception.

But the most important damage to them is to cause you to reject God's love, and God's way, and to end up in the same place with them.

Holy angels also present the life matters of the children of God before God on a regular basis. As an example, Jesus said, "Take heed that ye despise not one of these little ones; for I say unto you, That in heaven their angels do always behold the face of my Father which is in heaven" (Matthew 18:10). These activities are not a waste of their time and efforts; they are so that God can do something for them, so that God can give the go-ahead for them to make withdrawals from the treasury of God on their behalf. They take the prayer and praise of saints to God.

On the day of your trial, you will be judged for everything you did during your human lifetime. Everything will be brought up, everything! The good, the bad: every action, and every intention, worth being tried for.

These will be brought up:

- everything you said and the motive:
  Jesus said, "But I say unto you, That every idle word that men shall speak, they shall give account thereof in the day of judgment." Matthew 12:36
- everything you did and the motive.
- everything you did compared to the law of God.
- everything you did compared to the mercy of God.

The most important thing God will be looking for is how much you were to the centre of God's will. God will be the main Plaintiff on your big day, but in His love, He always gives a warning: "Say unto them, As I live, saith the Lord GOD, I have no pleasure in the death of the wicked; but that the wicked turn from his way and live: turn ye, turn ye from your evil ways; for why will ye die…" (Ezekiel 33:11).

You cannot escape the trial: "And as it is appointed unto men once to die, but after this the judgment…" (Hebrews 9:27). It is talking about every person, male and female, young and old: every ruler, every famous person, every rich person, every poor person, every responsible person, every not-so-responsible person, and every non-responsible person.

Chapter 2

THE TRIAL

There will be two kinds of the trial, of which you will attend only one, as the defendant. You cannot attend both. You cannot escape one or the other. God designed it.

The two kinds of the trial are:

- The judgment seat of Christ, and
- The great white throne judgment

THE JUDGMENT SEAT OF CHRIST

This is the trial only for the people that maintained innocence with God during their earthly life time. They maintain innocence with God through the atonement, and following God's way. Because of God's holiness, the atonement is God's means by which we may start to have a loving relationship with Him. The atonement is the means by which God imputes innocence. (Please see the yellow book. The atonement is explained in it and how it is enjoyed).

Paul wrote to people who have been declared righteous with God, through the saviour Jesus, saying, "for we shall all stand before the judgment seat of Christ.
For it is written, As I live, saith the Lord, every knee shall bow to me, and every tongue shall confess to God.
So then every one of us shall give account of himself to God." Romans 14:11-12

The purpose of the judgment seat of Christ is to determine the following, to last forever:

- Rewards, for actively serving God. Read these statements by Paul: "Now he that planteth and he that watereth are one: and every man shall receive his own reward according to his own labour.
  For we are labourers together with God: ye are God's husbandry, *ye are* God's building.
  According to the grace of God which is given unto me, as a wise masterbuilder, I have laid the foundation, and another buildeth thereon. But let every man take heed how he buildeth thereupon.
  For other foundation can no man lay than that is laid, which is Jesus Christ.
  Now if any man build upon this foundation gold, silver, precious stones, wood, hay, stubble;
  Every man's work shall be made manifest: for the day shall declare it, because it shall be revealed by fire; and the fire shall try every man's work of what sort it is.

If any man's work abide which he hath built thereupon, he shall receive a reward.
If any man's work shall be burned, he shall suffer loss: but he himself shall be saved; yet so as by fire." I Corinthians 3:8-15

- Rewards, for actively obeying God. Read these statements by the Christ:

"To him that overcometh will I give to eat of the tree of life, which is in the midst of the paradise of God." Revelation 2:7

"He that overcometh shall not be hurt of the second death." Revelation 2:11

"To him that overcometh will I give to eat of the hidden manna, and will give him a white stone, and in the stone a new name written, which no man knoweth saving he that receiveth *it*." Revelation 2:17

- Rank and position, in the everlasting government of God.

"And he that overcometh, and keepeth my works unto the end, to him will I give power over the nations…" Revelation 2:26

> "He that overcometh, the same shall be clothed in white raiment; and I will not blot out his name out of the book of life, but I will confess his name before my Father, and before his angels." Revelation 3:5

> "Him that overcometh will I make a pillar in the temple of my God, and he shall go no more out: and I will write upon him the name of my God, and the name of the city of my God, *which is* new Jerusalem, which cometh down out of heaven from my God: and *I will write upon him* my new name." Revelation 3:12

> "To him that overcometh will I grant to sit with me in my throne, even as I also overcame, and am set down with my Father in his throne." Revelation 3:21

THE GREAT WHITE THRONE JUDGMENT

This is the trial only for the people that did not have innocence with God during their earthly life time, and the ones that did not maintain innocence with God.

Up till the time God presses the button (speaking figuratively) to end this age, living people will, by their own choosing, continue to receive salvation, if they have never been saved. Jesus Christ is God's current and ultimate means to provide for this:

"That if thou shalt confess with thy mouth the Lord Jesus, and shalt believe in thine heart that God hath raised him from the dead, thou shalt be saved.
For with the heart man believeth unto righteousness; and with the mouth confession is made unto salvation." Romans 10:9-10

It is possible to loose salvation during earthly life. Peter wrote about this: "For if after they have escaped the pollutions of the world through the knowledge of the Lord and Saviour Jesus Christ, they are again entangled therein, and overcome, the latter end is worse with them than the beginning.
For it had been better for them not to have known the way of righteousness, than, after they have known *it,* to turn from the holy commandment delivered unto them." 2 Peter 2:20-21

The great white throne is the seat of the Judge on the day of the great white throne judgment: "And I saw a great white throne, and him that sat on it, from whose face the earth and the heaven fled away; and there was found no place for them.
And I saw the dead, small and great, stand before God; and the books were opened: and another book was opened, which is *the book* of life: and the dead were judged out of those things which were written in the books, according to their works.
And the sea gave up the dead which were in it; and death and hell delivered up the dead which were in them: and they were judged every man according to their works.

And death and hell were cast into the lake of fire. This is the second death.
And whosoever was not found written in the book of life was cast into the lake of fire." Revelation 20:11-15

The main thing that will be brought up in this judgment is the non-acceptance of God's love. God's love made Him to institute the ministry of reconciliation for every person, whosoever will, to enjoy it.

Chapter 3

THE JUDGE & LAW

The Judge in the coming trial is Jesus Christ. God has given Jesus many responsibilities. Peter tells us about Jesus being the Judge: "And he commanded us to preach unto the people, and to testify that it is he which was ordained of God *to be* the Judge of quick and dead.
To him give all the prophets witness, that through his name whosoever believeth in him shall receive remission of sins." Acts 10:42-43

He will preside over the trial; He will ask for evidence and everything you will expect from a normal trial.

The law from which you will be tried is the law of God. The most popular place to find the law of God today is in the holy bible, and in your conscience, and through other words originating from God.

Before the bible was composed, God spoke His law directly to people.

The first law was to Adam and Eve: "And the LORD God commanded the man, saying, Of every tree of the garden thou mayest freely eat:
But of the tree of the knowledge of good and evil, thou shalt not eat of it: for in the day that thou eatest thereof thou shalt surely die." Genesis 2:16-17

The all-encompassing law is the law of love: Jesus said, "And thou shalt love the Lord thy God with all thy heart, and with all thy soul, and with all thy mind, and with all thy strength: this *is* the first commandment.
And the second *is* like, *namely* this, Thou shalt love thy neighbour as thyself. There is none other commandment greater than these" (Mark 12:30-31).

The law of God is also administered into our conscience by the Holy Spirit. We may not have seen it anywhere that it is not good to sleep with another man's wife, but we "know". We may not have seen it anywhere that it is not good to yield to temptation, but we "know".

It is possible to violate our conscience. It is possible to go far enough in this to make our "conscience seared" (1 Timothy 4:2).

Jesus Christ fulfilled all the laws of God. This is the reason "Christ *is* the end of the law for righteousness to every one that believeth" (Romans 10:4) in Him with appropriating faith.

Chapter 4

THE WITNESSES & EVIDENCE

The main witnesses at the trial are the holy angels assigned to every person at birth, till death. They record everything, and it is easy for them to do this.

Angel recordings will be used as undeniable evidence.

You are being watched by them. They see everything, they hear everything. They may not know the motive behind everything, but the Holy Spirit knows everything.

God sees everything: He said "Can any hide himself in secret places that I shall not see him? saith the LORD. Do not I fill heaven and earth? saith the LORD." Jeremiah 23:24

Chapter 5

THE DAY

Different people have put the day of the great white throne judgment in different ways:

"For the day of the LORD of hosts *shall be* upon every *one that is* proud and lofty, and upon every *one that is* lifted up; and he shall be brought low..." Isaiah 2:12

"For *it is* the day of the LORD's vengeance..." Isaiah 34:8

"Flee out of the midst of Babylon, and deliver every man his soul: be not cut off in her iniquity; for this *is* the time of the LORD's vengeance; he will render unto her a recompense." Jeremiah 51:6

"The days of visitation are come, the days of recompense are come... for the multitude of thine iniquity, and the great hatred." Hosea 9:7

"Alas for the day! for the day of the LORD *is* at hand, and as a destruction from the Almighty shall it come." Joel 1:15

"Blow ye the trumpet in Zion, and sound an alarm in my holy mountain: let all the inhabitants of the land tremble: for the day of the LORD cometh, for *it is* nigh at hand;

A day of darkness and of gloominess, a day of clouds and of thick darkness, as the morning spread upon the mountains: a great people and a strong; there hath not been ever the like, neither shall be any more after it, *even* to the years of many generations." Joel 2:1-2

"The sun shall be turned into darkness, and the moon into blood, before the great and the terrible day of the LORD come." Joel 2:31

"Before the decree bring forth, *before* the day pass as the chaff, before the fierce anger of the LORD come upon you, before the day of the LORD's anger come upon you." Zephaniah 2:2

On this day, some will curse God. Some will blaspheme. The worst of profane words will be directed at God on this day. Some will try to escape, but the angels will be on guard. Some will ask for pardon, but it will be too late.

You can only sign yourself up for a place with God during life on earth. (See chapter 6 of the orange book).

Chapter 6

THE REWARD & PUNISHMENT

The preceding chapters have touched on God's reward and punishment following the trials. Here are more on rewards or punishment from the trial.

After the judgment seat of Christ:

"...they that be wise shall shine as the brightness of the firmament; and they that turn many to righteousness as the stars forever and ever." Daniel 12:3

Some will receive heavenly crowns. (See chapter 31 of the green book).

Some will be Jesus Christ's closest companions: "These are they which follow the Lamb whithersoever he goeth. These were redeemed from among men, *being* the firstfruits unto God and to the Lamb.
And in their mouth was found no guile: for they are without fault before the throne of God." Revelation 14:4-5

After the great white throne judgment, the accused in this trial will "go into hell, into the fire that never shall be quenched:
Where their worm dieth not, and the fire is not quenched." Mark 9:43-44

Chapter 7

THE ENDLESS END

The end of the judgments will commence eternity.

It is up to you to determine which judgement you will face. It is up to you to determine the quality of your eternity. Now is your chance to do something about it.

The outcome of the judgments will determine your endless end: your forever.

Applying the atonement, and not loosing this blessing, is prerequisite to eternity at home with God.

This is one of the Christian foundation books.

The Christian foundation books: MIGHTY MESSAGES BY INSPIRATION OF THE CHRIST are

- A last prayer (or a most important prayer): to avoid double death (red book)
- A lifestyle of love: A power of God at work in you (pink book)
- Take favour: Access to the life God composed for you (orange book)
- What it is to be born again (yellow book)
- We are blessed: An exposé of the life God proposed for you (green book)
- Sword of the Spirit (series) (blue book)
- The Person of Almighty God (purple book)
- Holiness (white book)
- Spirits affect you: Spirits of God & spirits of devils (grey book)
- The Coming trial: You cannot escape it (black book)

Information about other books by A.A.O.Olatunde are available at www.thechristianfoundationbooks.com

Made in the USA
Monee, IL
04 November 2026

67386539R10015